all things said & done

MARITA DACHSEL

all things said & done

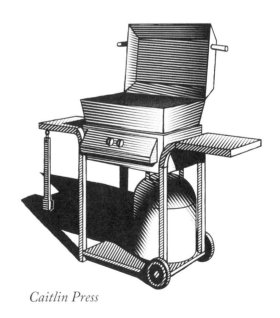

Caitlin Press

Caitlin Press
P.O. Box 219, Madeira Park, BC, V0N 2H0
www.caitlin-press.com

Edited by Silas White
Cover illustration by Drew Kennickell
Cover and page design by Anna Comfort
Printed in Canada

Caitlin Press acknowledges financial support from the Government of Canada through the Book Publishing Industry Development Program and the Canada Council for the Arts, and from the Province of British Columbia through the BC Arts Council and the Book Publishing Tax credit.

Library and Archives Canada Cataloguing in Publication

Dachsel, Marita

All things said and done / Marita Dachsel.

Poems.

ISBN-13: 978-1-894759-22-9
ISBN-10: 1-894759-22-2

I. Title.
PS8557.A263A75 2006 C811'.54 C2006-906958-1

for my family

CONTENTS

ONE:
small-town breeding

Fish Stories

I

How to clean a fish:

1. Insert the knife through the anus.
2. With the blade, follow, but do not cut, the spine.
3. Scoop out the organs in one motion.
4. Rinse the insides clean.

This is one thing my father taught me.

II

When I was eight, my friends and I would search through garbage cans at the cleaning hut in search of fish heads. We would take what we could carry to our secret fort behind the cabins, down the beach, near a stream. Once there, we would take turns using the blunt end of an axe to smash open the heads, hoping to find the grey pea-sized brain of the fish. If you didn't do it right, the brain would smush and you would lose. Our intentions childish, a contest to see whose collection of fish brains would be largest at the close of the summer. That never happened. The crows always came and stole them after we were called to supper.

III

The gills were still moving when my father inserted his knife and slid it through the fish. He didn't know this, he wasn't cruel, he would have clubbed its head before slicing it open. But when he scooped out the organs he saw the heart still pumping. He said nothing but held it for a moment and then placed it in my open palm.

FLIGHT

Flight for her
is not a matter of how, but when.
She will push up through the sky,
her fingers hooking clouds
that taste like birthday cake icing.
Her legs will pump easy
like in the water where
she spends her summers practising.

Long before puberty, there are things
she knows: she will not change
her name when she marries,
she will never stomach liver,
she will leave this town, go
far far away.

After school she visits
travel agencies to steal brochures
dense with photographs
and simplified maps,
coloured trajectories
leading the way.
She collages everything
in her possession.

Outside Overwaitea
she rides the 25-cent horse
bucking, wildly inert
the mechanical whirr gallops her
to an impossible horizon.

In grade six she learns
elementary cartography,
she sketches mountains
instead of doodling,
creates gradients
sheer cliffs, deadly faces.

Daily, she plots escape
over the valley hands
limp in rock—a marionette
holding her stationary.

SUMMER SCARS

I was fourteen and tanning was still cool
the summer I stole the rusted lure
from my father's tackle box.

My friends and I scratched
the names of the boys we loved
on each other's arms and bellies—

the barbed hook etched,
leaving our warmed brown skin scarred
until winter faded everything away.

DEER IN THE CARPORT

At minus fifteen, the deer carcass
is hung in the carport so it won't rot,
but it must be strung high enough
or the neighbour's dogs
will steal what they can.

My parents saw through lumps
of muscle, one section at a time.
They have spread newspapers on the floor,
counter and kitchen table, but the blood
always puddles through.

My parents are happy
when they slice up the deer.
The meat will last until summer.

But I want it to come clean from the store,
sandwiched between white Styrofoam
and tight plastic with no stench
that clings to clothes and prompts
the kids at school to scrunch their noses
and ask, *What smells funny?*

Book Club

It was luck, lifting that
book from that pile.

She was twelve years old and her mother
was just happy she was reading,

never once picking it up
thinking of a need to censor

the glossy novel pulp and brash.
Americans in India, drugs and sexploitation,

but more with the stomach warming
as the cobra, enchanted,

charmed its way up the legs of enraptured
women, tongue forked and ecstatic:

> A question for her mother:
> *What does an orgasm feel like?*

> A puzzled answer for the daughter:
> *Oh, you'll know when you have one.*

Dogs became lovers, horses
were revered, orgies abounded,

sections dog-eared for easy
reference, until finished and satisfied

she brought the book to school,
meant it to be read aloud

in small groups behind the portable,
recess and lunch hours curried heat.

But soon it was borrowed, as casual
weekend reading, handed out indiscriminately.

She loses the book, as is bound to happen.
She will lose many things over the years

       but some things remain: she often
       calls her first college boyfriend

       by her dog's name, considers the practicality
       of owning a snake, learns dressage

and the warm remembering of last night's dream—
vast tongues, four-legged fur and muscle

—the unmistakable pulsing her awake,
reaching to her subcontinent for more.

SAFETY IN NUMBERS

Ours was a house obsessed
with buttons. Mom most of all:
Don't press your father's buttons.

He sure knows how to— But we
didn't detonate. No explosions
shook the neighbours,

or mushroom clouds seen
from the next town over.
No debris or chaos.

Just a small slow death.
Milk souring. Floorboards rotting.
A caught thread unravelling.

SALINAS

I dream of Steinbeck, knowing he would have been a great lover. He would have never taken me to the dump to get naked in the back of a greasy orange Chevy truck with a bald spare tire for my head to bang against. No, he would have taken me to a secret field full of yellow poppies and blue flowers iced in white. He would have gently lain me down on a flannel blanket instead of pulling me up the tailgate onto the towel you use to wipe the windshield. He would have caressed me, tickled my arm, and kissed my neck before touching my blouse which you require off before you can kiss me. He would have whispered, *We have an audience*, and laughed at the curious birds, never swearing at the crows during the middle of it. And Steinbeck would never have demanded to do it in the back of his truck while his buddies sat in the front drinking cheap beer.

QUIETLY

This is how I remember her: dancing
feverish to Run DMC at the wedding
reception for Sheryl and Wayne, one ankle
sprained, limbs sinewy, strength cultivated
from a summer of reforestation, browned
like a perfect marshmallow.

Sure, she had crazy eyes, but we all did
exhausted from small-town breeding,
our bodies releasing everything
with the aid of the open bar
and confetti swirls.

None could suspect how things would turn
out, that the marriage would crumble
before the second anniversary. None could
guess that she, electric, buzzing to be spent,
would end it quietly with only the kick
of a stool and the rope around exposed pipe
tensing against her weight.

New Year's Eve, 1996

In the truck, he is trying to tell
the two women a story he knows they
have already heard, a story he will tell
them again in variations throughout the night:
the death of his best friend a year ago yesterday.

He tries to explain that he had never cried
before, but now anything will set him off—
hearing his best friend's favourite song,
remembering how his father cried
when the family dog died.

The truck falls silent and only
the sound of the rye and Coke bottles
clinking in his lap is heard, muffled slightly
by his winter jacket arms cuddling
the contents of the brown paper bag.

He looks at the snow outside—
a satin mattress full of down. He looks at
the shadows the streetlight makes, and back
at the women, their eyes fixed where his were,
they are both contemplating something different.

There is a party inside that the women
are anxious to join, to leave behind his talk of death.
But even in their loud and furious countdown
with kisses frenzied like the snowstorm outside
this moment will remain, a scratched record playing.

I Have a Hole in My Head

I can't see it, but others can:
a small black scab—
a dead spider, a bullet tip—
unnatural against my pale scalp.

*

I have a hole in my head
(this isn't about suicide).

*

In my blind prodding
it feels huge, the healing coarse.
I constantly threaten to nick it away,
welcome the blood warm and sticky.

*

I have a hole in my head
(this isn't about suicide,
but it could be).

*

I want my finger to core
past the itch, behind the healing.
If I try hard enough,
I imagine I could reach skull.

*

I have a hole in my head
(this isn't about suicide,
but it could be—
almost everything is).

on bedding she would never want to own
a mattress that is not hers, frayed flannel sheets
greyed from too many washings, a red wool blanket,
an afghan someone's aunt crocheted with love

she takes in the man above her, opening
shutting her eyes like a camera lens
creating a scrapbook of images
to remember the thinning blond hair

uneven skin of an acned youth
orthodontist-approved teeth
tar-stained and caffeinated
nose broken from a drunken teenage fight

he tells her to play with her tits, it turns him on
in her head she tells him to
fuck off, fuck you
and shakes her head no

instantly she begins to forget his name
but wraps her legs around his pelvis
runs her fingers down his back
sharp and fierce, vowing to break skin

STINGS

She had been negligent,
missing the blue pills days in a row.
This morning, in prickling false relief, she
mistook spotting for an early period.
She knows this can happen,
she's watched enough television
to know what this could mean.

(the dust on the candles spark)

Water stings, the heat
of the bath is too much
but she lowers herself
shrouding her body
under the waterline.
Arching her back, she pushes
the bump of her stomach
exaggerated out,
shadowed large.

NORTHERN LOVE

She will admit that she has been here too long.
Her judgement gone like the tundra,
permafrost melted under heavy
days, unending sunlight—
uneven, bumpy
illogically untraversable.
It's the men here: beards
she finds sexy. And the guys
who glint are large out of necessity
and heavy drinking, having downed
bears and heavy moose.

She has a longing—her intestines
unravelled, tugging her along—
for a man you can tell has killed
just by looking at him, who knows
instinctively how to butcher and skin,
mounts antlers above the door to his home.
She wants a man who keeps his fingernails
clean despite no running water,
and has dug his own outhouse;
who once ran a trapline
but now considers the benefits
of tourism: dogsleds and snowmobiles.
His truck smells like oil,
dog and dirt, and when she drives
with him down to Whitehorse
his eyes well up at the sight of the mountain
blazed purple with fireweed.

Odds are against this union, but she has a hunch
that it will last. He will grow much older
much sooner than she will and she will lose him
piece by piece, slowly. His teeth will rot,
fall out, but he will keep a head
of thick hair silvered and coarse. His body will shrink,
his skin hanging off like a billowy veil.
Frostbite will steal a few toes. He may
accidentally lop a finger while chopping firewood.
She will order fancy creams to keep
her appearance young, but her mind will go
long before his and by the end, neither
will recognize the other. She knows this
and it still makes her happy. She will hold
him, stake and claim him, while waiting
for the inevitable lightless days.

IN BED

she curls herself
a baby shrimp up against him
tight inside his parenthetical body
she searches his chest for greying hair
lazy fists raised in reluctant salute

combing through, she knows three
and finds a fourth a finger-width
below his left nipple
she fills with hot chocolate warmth
she is the guardian of this

his tiny hairs shudder against her lips
as she whispers to his sternum
asking if it may be she who will witness
this patch of him coil slowly old and grey

Game Plan

He will avoid the bridesmaids
festooned in taffeta and satin, dresses
cut on the wrong side of ugly, too worried
about being captured in albums, on mantles
to focus on anything but a smudge in their makeup
and sucking their stomachs taut.

He will find the woman, perhaps a cousin of the groom
or an out-of-city, losing-touch-with friend of the bride,
who will be taking full advantage
of the open bar, mocking the buffet, collecting
bets on which of the uncles will pass out first
and firmly giving the couple three years max.

She in the dress with a neckline a little too low,
heels an inch too high, will be an optimist
with four condoms in her purse. He knows
she will fuck as well as she dances, give the best head,
and will hold him tight, breath soft on the back of his neck,
through the night and well past morning.

SUITCASE

She says:
I can fit into a suitcase
(like sperm in a condom, like you in my bed)
I can reduce my life to a handful
of matching separates, two bathing suits,
sunscreen, hiking books, sandals.

She says:
I can go anywhere anytime
give me an hour to pack
and to make my way to the airport
and I'm gone, goodbye, outta here.

She says:
I am happiest living nearly naked,
the smell of sunscreen is an aphrodisiac,
I need to be near water, to feel
its movement calming my organs.

He watches her standing naked
at the foot of their bed, nipples erect,
a pimple forming on her neck
as she flattens her manic hair,
staring back at him, daring a response.

He pulls her back to bed and says:
it's coconut oil, not sunscreen, that turns you on
and you could spend an hour in traffic alone,
(you should give yourself more time to pack)
and it's the big things that weigh heavy,
that slip in, invisible.

TWO:
all things said & done

Mrs. Torrance

You were doomed from the beginning.
Your son, at five, is smarter than you.
Pink and gold is an awful combination.
Your husband, Mrs. Torrance, your husband
has anger-management issues, and surely
you are already aware that temperance
isn't working well for him:
he will sell his soul for a drink.
Send him up to the mountains
with a case of bourbon and his precious
typewriter, ship your son to grandma's.
Treat yourself to a haircut and a new dress,
you need to go dancing, where you can
flail under the sharp-edged disco lights.

MISCELLANY: NOT A NEWS STORY

She stood in front of the Degas ballerina
for almost an hour. You noticed this only because
this is your favourite section: young women
in various stages of undress, muscles sore
and strong, flexing into stances of beauty and pain.

She spent an hour completing the orbit
around the ballerina. This was no way to tackle
the Met—you told her this during the announcement
for closing. She looked at you blankly and shrugged,
There's nothing else worth seeing. You guffawed,
then winced at the loud reminder of your Texas roots.

Giggling, she asked your name. This was your first
mistake, the moment where everything changed. A man
of your intelligence knows that choice reveals all intent,
as unconscious as it may have been at the time. Was it the thrill
of being an unknown again, a throwback to your youth?

As you scanned the room, dismissing the Impressionists
as too obvious—*You? French?*—your gaze settled
on an Upper West Side socialite and her oversized handbag.
Today, you wonder if the outcome would have been different
if you'd chosen Cole instead of Kenneth. Would somehow the other
have offered less suspicion, seemed less of a threat?

On the massive front steps, you asked her if she'd be interested
in a drink; she suggested ice cream. Later, you stressed
to your therapist the important difference between a simpleton
and an innocent. Her smiling face, large and open, always
on the verge of laughter or a question that invariably made you think.

The frequency of your meetings increased after the walk
through Central Park when you kissed her for the first time
under the shadow of William Shakespeare. You finally
knew what love could be. You had told her your dream was
to work at Rockefeller Center; hers was to be a lift operator
in the Empire State Building. She loved elevators.

You must have suspected she was underage, that her soft flesh
was virginal, but that didn't stop you. Rather, you wanted nothing
more than having her in your bed and once you did,
you would frequently make love with her mid-morning, before
 you had to be at the office, preparing to face the sombre world
Did the relationship stop before the brothers found out?

Did they console your jilted lover and then come after you?
Or did they discover who her new boyfriend was by accidentally
watching the wrong nightly news as she swooned over a middle-aged
non-Kenneth? Or did you get her pregnant and the consequences
were more than either of you could bare? There were many
questions for you, though you were only asked the one,

on your way to a dinner party you could never bring your sweetheart to.
You, who knew the nuances of perception and biases in the news;
you, with a new face for America, were a changed man.
What was perceived as the discomfort of bruised ribs, the remembrance
of the bloodied face, the anxiousness of fear, was your new found
unhappiness and broken heart. You still walk past

the Empire State building with a tinge of remorse, take the stairs
rather than elevators, and have not returned to Degas or any
of the Europeans, preferring an afternoon with the Egyptians.
Although you have since given up the ineffective disguise of sunglasses
and ball cap, we the people can see through your steady voice, calm
demeanour, that you have not forgotten, and will not let go.

Driftwood

Because yet another friend was getting married he ventured into that artist-run gallery gift shop, wafting incense and flute music. He explained to the long-haired, beaded beauty—goddess behind the counter snapping peppermint gum—that he was looking for something original, made with love. He elongated *love*, in hopes that their eyes would meet in the saying, but she was too consumed with the cataloguing of wind chimes to look up once during his confession.

Upon purchasing her suggestion, a heavy pottery casserole and a cinnamon-and-clove-filled pot holder, he mentioned as if in passing that he too was an artist and was looking for an establishment of repute to sell his creations. Her interest stirred. So did he. He asked her to coffee. Then a movie. Then dinner. He said he was a *found folk artist*, and began to scour the beaches. He bought a hot glue gun.

While collecting debris, he questioned his choice of commuting downtown, a desk from nine to six. He stopped cutting his hair. He had lots of sex. He explained his art was *a dialogue between nature and consumerism, ecology and materialism.* When showing his sculptures (made quickly, calling in sick for two days straight) for the first time, he shrugged off the disappointment in her face, fully aware of his toothbrush leaning against hers. He knew it was just junk glued to driftwood (Barbie parts and gum wrappers became his favourite materials) and said, *It's the process that's beautiful*, and, *You inspire me.* His happiness overflowed: he had lots of sex.

KEMANO

He's lucked out with a phone in his room,
calls his wife two, three times a day,
likes to listen to her chew leftover roast beef,
scalloped potatoes. They talk about nothing,
just like when they first started going out,
before the three kids, mortgage, this job.

Six days on, seven off, twelve-hour shifts
in this working ghost town, sixteen clicks
to the ocean and mountain bases two strides away.
Off the phone he spends the non-working hours
with the guys in the pool room
just drinking Kokanee and shooting the shit.

Last night his wife asked
if he ever sees the old home. *Nah,*
he lied, picking at his ripped cuticle,
everything's all boarded up, nothing to see…
an overgrown garden, a rotting porch.
She sighed, *Kenny learned to walk on that porch.*

On the bus to the Helijet at the end of
these six days they are driven their weekly route,
past the old neighbourhood. His buddy elbows him
and points, *that one yours?* and he watches
the plastic siding curl upwards like fingernails
collapsing his burning home as the fire crews practise,
careful to leave only charred shadows.

A Choice

Fly fishing may be the most romantic:
the long malleable rod, the line teasing
the surface, wading submerged to the hips,
the river's current a nudging reminder
of where the power is possessed.

And deep-sea fishing may be the sexiest
under the tropical sun, requiring straps and pulleys,
a fight and a team to bring a monster in,
then to be stuffed, displayed at the best vantage,
compliments easily reeled in.

But he prefers trolling, a mid-powered Johnson
behind him, guiding across the lake, low stakes
may equal low rewards, but he enjoys trout for dinner,
a pretty changing view, dry feet and the pleasure
to fish with a rod in one hand, beer in the other.

Conduct

Oh, he has heard the jokes,
his wife gently nudging. He
knows the word *phallic*,
and what the tenants think
of his five-foot-two frame
blowing leaves daily through
the dry weeks of autumn.

But there is music beneath that motor.
Inaudible to the unrefined, that melodious
humming, the symphony of engines, pure
inspiration to the spastic ballet of debris.

Riches

And there is always the neighbour
up at 6 a.m. on weekends, metal
detector in hand, certain his fortune
will come from the clumsy
carelessness of others.

(Never once the suspicion
that the 1918 Buffalo coin
found with his father at age eleven
was staged, a well-intentioned set-up.)

He has a plan.

Retirement will come sooner: cartoon
easiness with ruby rings, diamond
tennis bracelets, rare foreign coins
will be his archaeological finds,
this man and his divining rod.

STORIES

Underfoot, crushing the skull
of a chipmunk found suffering,
giving way like a jawbreaker
candied thin, the gum centre busting

or

saving a friend from drowning in late October,
the river dangerously cold, a deceptive undertow,
fighting to find shore two kilometres downstream,
the hospital night spent together
under hypothermia watch.

(These are stories to tell
in the presence of women
made to feel privileged
by tales of small bones, fast water
in spite of lipstick and underwear
made difficult with hooks and clasps.)

But the men will not say
even to each other, despite
the amount of Scotch consumed,

that the chipmunk was fallen
on purpose by his BB gun

&

that it was his well-placed shin
that sent the friend tumbling,

all accompanied with laughter
rumbling pure and snide.

Over Mid-Morning Coffee and a Magazine, He Mourns the Loss of Corporal Punishment and the Stolen Fantasies of Subsequent Generations

His own he doubts he could manufacture, his
imagination potent enough only to refine
the memory of his naughtiness,
an ecstatic bad boy, bare ass over
the desk, with the glimpse of demure
dark nylons, the rupture of a run
at the heel, modest in two-inch pumps.

Without it, he questions whether the presence
of a yardstick or the intoxicating perfume
of chalk dust could still evoke such tingling joy.
As he closes his eyes to the slap
of a hand, hairbrush or spatula
it is forever grade three and Miss Brown
not so gingerly conceiving the blows.

Remembering

Lying in bed, he watches his naked wife
apply cocoa butter cream to her cellulite
and twenty-five-year-old stretch marks.
He, with hands resting on his stomach,
large—admittedly from his love of beer
and his wife's perogies—is remembering.
They have just returned from his wife's thirtieth
high school reunion, where he endured the awkward
flirting between her and her now completely
bald, big-teeth-dentured high school sweetheart,
and now he is remembering the summer after graduation:

A warm skinned Mediterranean August, a girl
from Turkey all curved and velvet touch, lost
in spiced alcohol and foreign fruit. Even now,
surrounded by Sears decor and a generation
of family portraits, he can conjure the scent
of that early afternoon and see that exact shade
of her toenails painted red which he studied
as she explained in accented English why
she needed the last of his travellers cheques,
and wonders now what she did with the money,
and for the first time, if she truly was pregnant.

Gardening Is a Pointless Hobby

He knows it's been such a waste—all that exertion
and time, back strained and dirtied fingers for his wife.
Her fleeting, transparent joy in announcing
smugly to the luncheon guests that the whole salad—
tomatoes, leafy lettuce, radishes and carrots
(which he hates in salads, but the wife would grate
them for show, for colour, for bulk)—that the whole
salad came directly from their very own garden.

He has never been interested in gardening—flowers
might be pretty to the wife, but ultimately useless,
and produce, well don't get him started on produce.
His grandparents were farmers and he believes
that produce can't be done half-heartedly. The season
must include canning, jamming and pickling,
or you may as well find yourself at the Safeway
picking through bruised tomatoes and wilted lettuce.

But it seems, as most things do now, that he has little
choice. Herded into the garden when he'd rather
be watching *Antiques Roadshow*. Year after year,
holiday after holiday, opening well-taped parcels
of gardening utensils, books and accessories. So,
to his wife's dismay, he has unearthed the bulbs, eradicated
the flowerbeds, dug up the fancy tomatoes and beans.
He will plant nothing except a summer of cabbage—
        revenge
will permeate. They will wade through months of coleslaw
and sauerkraut, uneasy digestions and unfortunate farts.

Holiday Cheer

There is no holiday more dismal than Christmas.
With the ripping of cheerful red and green

patterned wrap, you hope that this year,
this time, just this once, your children

will have chosen with thought and love
something you may actually like,

or have at least shown interest in.
Nevertheless, disappointment overrides.

But your grown children—who still
write *Daddy* on the label, who spent

their formative years under the same roof
in the same house you provided for

—know you so little. Every year you expect
that when they look at you with their unblinking eyes,

they will suddenly transform into windup plush toys
that yelp and do flips and prove they really are of no use at all.

THERE WERE BETTER TIMES THAN THESE

He has already made the switch from beer to red wine having paid attention during the medical segments on the nightly news.

Over the roar of the barbecue, he takes stock.

His daughter in the kitchen refilling the neighbour's drinks, his wife skilfully mingling, laughing at the boss's jokes, sharing her recipe for low-fat coleslaw (appropriated from last month's *Chatelaine*). And there is his son,

feet away crouching on concrete, defacing the freshly cleaned siding with a stolen lipstick (not his wife's demure pink, but a shocking coral). He knows he should say something, stop the boy.

As he peels the plastic off perfect, square cheese slices he contemplates what to do with the knowledge that charcoal causes cancer but whitens teeth, and that studies have shown that cheeseburgers increase heart disease but reduce cancer.

Dabbling in medical science is, he is discovering, fruitless.

Globs of cheese drop, flare then extinguish. Watching his son's slick figures jaunt obscene on this corner of the house, he is certain that there were better times than these.

WEEKEND IN KAMLOOPS

Backing into the driveway, I see
the neighbour across the street
peer out the window, calculating—
he knows your parents are in Japan
visiting friends who once slept
in the bedroom we will share. We are castaways
curled up, taking in the sagebrushed view
from across the Thompson, hills folded,
layers dusted by the Shuswap, where
the mornings rise with a murmuration of starlings.

You find the keys to your father's pickup
and suddenly I become giddy. You open
the door for me and sliding in, I ask
if you want me to sit beside you.
We both laugh knowing
this small-town shorthand.

This is a dress rehearsal, playing house
at your parents'. We use appliances,
build a fire, play board games,
go to bed early. At dinner, I cry
to a Neil Young song and wonder,
Am I draining you?—how you fill me
to bursting and still have
the energy to go on.

AIRPORT MUSIC
after Charles Baxter

We have overpacked again.
The straps already straining our shoulders,
our lower backs already tiring to the weight
and we are only in the airport.

We haven't checked in yet, but are standing
at the concourse window, coffees in hand,
watching the take-offs

                the arrivals.
(those flying tins full
of expectancy)

We know we could put the packs down,
save our bodies, but somehow that would feel like cheating.

We are silently listening for it.

                      We can't hear it,
but we feel it—that airport music—a pop tune
that never leaves us,
            infecting,
                humming
inside for so long we can't tell the difference
between it and our own beating hearts.

We have been on many trips without the other,
but now that seems inconceivable.
                              Why
would I venture anywhere without you—
my perfect travelling partner,
                              my journeying companion?

I am here and I want to take your hand,
but I don't. There is no need to.
You know I am here. We are ready to go.

DISPATCHES FROM AN IMPENDING MARRIAGE

Take this razor & slice the soles of my feet.
Careful.
        Roll me out of my skin.
                Gentle.
I am a silk stocking.
I am your joy.

*

You are a fool
to keep the bathroom window open
in weather like this.

The tub is much too cold

even water that should be scalding
can't lift the chill from the porcelain.

*

Don't talk to me about photographers.
Nothing will capture this. A printed paper
will only mock—
           a gaudy misrepresentation
           a plastic Jesus on the mantle—
two dimensions of fabric, teeth & skin.

*

It is not that we are too tired for sex.
No. It is something else completely.

*

Please let me burrow in there. Yes, there
right below your sternum.

Let me core into you.
                    Infest.

*

We share soaps & lotions,
an alchemy of scents.
But it is not enough to smell the same.

*

A misplaced nail clipping.
I try to slip it under my skin,

a moon-shaped nub of you at my wrist
(instead, I ingest you
                    nibble, nibble
swallow).

*

There is talk about the stove.

I was told the new gas ones
have a safety on them to prevent—

you assure me ours is too old.
It does not.

*

Try this:
        inhale. Slow, deep, aggressive.

Snort me in scalp-first.
I can fit.
        There will be room
        for two.

THREE:
uncharted territory

STOCKHOLM SYNDROME

her impatience is an unreachable
hair caught between shoulder blades
she needs
sunshine, heat, the sweet discomfort
of a slight sunburn
she wants
his full affection, tender kisses, love
will come under a star-freckled desert night
she knows
a kidnap of his attention, forcing
the weekend captive, a brainwash body
wash away any reservations

in the intimacy of a DC-10
they share mini-pretzels, middle names
a game of hangman
she loses to
milk fed boys are groovy
and *xanadu,* but happiness blooms
despite her haggling over rules

Route 7

With *Fodor's 2000 New Mexico* and *Compass American Guides: Santa Fe* on the back seat, useless now that they are crossing into Arizona, she has balanced *Hidden Southwest, Compass American Guides: The American Southwest* and Triple A's fold-out map of the Western States/Provinces on her knees.

(sweating despite the air conditioning,
she's never been good at navigation,
her last boyfriend
read the maps as she drove;
now, in a state of panic, she just
doesn't want to *fuck up*)

Somewhere between Grant and Gallup, she reads aloud from the guides and shows him the pictures on straight stretches. They decide to head to Monument Valley by way of Canyon De Chelly.

(his baseline headache
strums flat and throbbing,
he needs caffeine
now, now, *now*)

They stop in Window Rock for coffee (she thought they had already passed through). They are in Hopi land and they talk politics. She's sure the Republicans will win, he has more faith in the American public. After her second cup she excuses herself to use the restroom. When she's gone, he steals a look at her cache, studies the inky jumble on the Triple A, and upon her return he suggests Route 7, a dirt road not mentioned in any of the guides. Relieved, she eagerly agrees.

(he's wary of her travel-guide obsession,
is this, he wonders,
how she goes through life,
a perpetual self-helper?)

An hour lost in Fort Defiance, stumbling down dead ends,
up driveways trying to find the mouth of their unmarked
way, until they trip over the dusty shoelace road. The route
is bumpy and deserted, the only movement is their curling
plume behind them, and when the road forks, there are no
signs. They take turns choosing, right, left, then left again, and
each hopes the other will trust their instincts.

THE ANTELOPE HOUSE OVERLOOK

We stand on the pastry crust
of this unfinished sculpture
miles in size
monumental walls of rust
sliced and polished pillars
moulded, caves and crevasses chiselled away
the debris scattered, discarded rubble
on the valley floor a green violent gash.

We hear hammering reverberate
through the valley, origin unknown,
a site of distant echoes.

I point out across the valley
an archaeology
of white antelopes, their chalky shadows
loom above an Anasazi home left
in a state of elapsed energy
hand-formed, sun-dried, crafted
one brick at a time, a built excavation.

You tell me of a bowl
thrown on a wheel
ancient palms that formed a perfect vessel
with an unbreakable groove
from the base to the lip
circling, hugging the bowl, a caress found
in the hands of science, with technology, little
advanced from a turntable and a sophisticated needle
played only once, emitting sounds captured
for over a thousand years:
muffled voices, wailing baby, a barking dog.

We marvel at science and sound
and I wonder could it capture this:
the largeness of this valley, the heavy heat,
my hand inching toward yours.

WEST FROM ALBUQUERQUE

Route 66
a scattering of miles, a strip
of gas stations, diners
and Americana clichés.
West from Albuquerque
we stop for burritos.

A pair of state troopers flirt with the waitress
as she pours our coffee bitter black.
Wood panelling, a stuffed armadillo,
mirrored beer plaques—we hold this,
cupping memories that will slip through our fingers,
loose sugar blown off the Formica.

Super 8 in Grant, New Mexico,
two queen-sized beds
we fuck wet and aggressive
sweat and secretions move us
from one bed to the other.
The toilet runs all night.
You snore as I trace the relief
of the freckles on your back.

MONUMENT VALLEY CAMPGROUND

Just past dusk we roll into the campground.
We are shades of grey, grainy like found footage
setting up your roommate's tent
green and well-adventured.

With the help of a Maglite
we discover our site is flat but all rock and dust
like the surrounding dark-shadowed high slab walls.
Our borrowed Thinsulates will help little tonight.

The army of stars is brighter than
my city-numbed self can remember.
As I search for the Big Dipper I realize
tonight will be the first time I have sex in a tent.

I want to echo through this valley,
be as American as possible: brash and proud,
summoning my manifest destiny, ignoring
the thin tarp that will separate us from them.

FALLOUT

Things are different here.

At first, we attribute
it to our exhaustion,

the front desk waking
us, calling three times:

will we be checking out,
when do we expect to check out,
checkout is at eleven o'clock.

At noon, we return our keys,
join the Sunday Brunch Buffet

in the finely upholstered dining room.

Father's Day: balding men dominate
crisp bacon, congealing eggs,

pancakes at room temperature.
We are in the minority,

not part of this demographic, fathers
our fathers' age, taking out their fathers.

Even the waitresses are wrinkled,
liverspotted since the fifties.

Just after we both vow to call
our own fathers, you lean into me

whisper *Oppenheimer* then *Fat Man,
Manhattan Project.* I look at you

and you nod towards the room, the deteriorating
men who once changed the world.

At the Bradbury Science Museum,
your delight transports us, we are

children in awe playing with the exhibits
watching reels, filling ourselves

with post-war optimism.

After almost an hour in the gift shop,
a mug and magnet paper-bagged,

we agree that this is what we loved the best:
the few minutes of footage of young

bare-chested boys running around
the Los Alamos Ranch School, forced

to close when the government moved in,
a dozen boys drying off from an afternoon

swim, movement brisk, with just the blush
of pubescent awkwardness taking hold.

Haida Gwaii

I

It is the air we notice first,
and inhale deeply, bringing the islands in our bodies;
it hurts the lungs being in an environment this clean,
this infused with cedar. Almost imperceptibly,
as if your skin is reaching, straining to touch the mist,
you appear to inflate, but it is more than that,
and for a few days, for the first and only time, I believe in auras.

Our first night we head to Grey Bay; along the way
there are deer dancing sassy beside the road,
bald eagles larger than I imagined they could be.

We find a site to set up camp.
The tent, all periwinkle and buttercup,
like in the catalogue, pitched
on a mattress of moss,
our first home, I allow myself to think.
While you collect firewood,
I reach back to my camp days
to light the fire from a single match.
Through smoke thick from the damp, I see you return
with a jumble of wooded debris triumphant
and I wish: let this be forever.

The light of released sparks mulls with embers,
August and the North, create a twilight alchemy.
We share stories of childhood, camping, science
and then watch the fire eat itself to ashes.

We make love, gentle, loud and earnest.
Later, we are buzzed awake by ravens flying low, as revenge
I'm sure, over the domed roof. The whooshing flap
of wings millimetres away from the tent, their cries meant to scare.
I can't sleep, hearing them scratch at the ground,
conspiring, loud and fiercely cawing
and I wonder what they want from me.
I shift under the sleeping bag, turn to you for comfort
my hand on your chest, head hidden
to conceal how frightened I've become.

I am running our of ways to tell you that I love you
before the words are going to spill out of my mouth.
I tell your skin in whispers,
trace the words on your back,
through squeezes and finger pressure
tap my own Morse code.

In Sandspit we rent kayaks,
map in hand, navigate tiny islands
scattered around the Strait.

Through the brush of an anonymous island
a doe and fawn watch our Plexiglas and Gore-Tex,
only a few strokes from shore, we are hushed into tableaux,
charmed at the strangeness of this meeting
until the deer grow bored and disappear
into the camouflage of the bush.

We find a beachy bay to lunch on smoked salmon and snow peas.
You collect flat rocks to skip, we each choose three
and compete. I am embarrassed having you
be the first man to out-skip me since puberty.

II

In search of what the guidebook promises
is the oldest canoe on the Islands, abandoned before completion,
we walk along an overgrown logging road
when a 1951 army-issue truck meets us.
A young Haida man named Clint, behind the wheel,
says he can show us a better canoe,
so we jump in and he takes us away.

There are the moments we allow—a release, a suspension
of the expected—to be led on the trust and intuition
that this will be worth it.

Down an impassable road, to a logged clearing,
on a small paththe air becomes unnaturally warm
like an exhaled breath in the shade.
My skin begins to tingle and I see you inhale deeply.
The fallen canoe, discovered five years ago, is iridescent with moss
lit by a spotlight through the towering cedar branches.
We see what once was, arrested development,
the trunk and the top of the tree is visible
all in one line with the unfinished canoe flowing
from the stump, between.

I am afraid to touch it,
that doing so would simply make it vanish
but I see you place your palm, almost petting
the canoe as you walk around it.

There are small saplings growing out of what would be the bow.
Clint rips them out as he ruminates
about the canoe and its history;
he is the vessel keeper, self-installed
to hold onto its stalled state.

I lightly touch the canoe,
the moss, dryer than I had expected,
the wood splintered and grey in places.
I feel like I am trespassing on interrupted potential.
I look up and see you watching me.

Later, we take one last walk on these islands
and find ourselves wearing silence
like a grey flannel blanket,
in an unending, secluded beach.

There is a rocky spit that leads to a point on the horizon,
and a curiosity pushes us down it.
I fall behind to watch you walk, navigating rock and water
as the tide comes in. I take in you, all, everything,
and suddenly I am overwhelmed
by our uncharted territory.

FLIGHT ATTENDANTS

Flight attendants don't age like the rest of us;
they are time travellers, smiling
purposefully at thirty thousand feet,
offering chicken or beef,
mixing the perfect Vodka 7
as they jump, passing through time zones
like earthbound mortals cross city streets.

MT. RUAPEHU, NZ

Just being in this country is putting my life at risk.
Travelling along the hump of a fault line
ready to suck me in or spurt me out;
there are places where the crust is so thin
mud boils and steam just appears.

Ahead of me your form falls
in and out of focus. The mist surrounds you
and I feel like I am in a movie
with overzealous special effects.

You have climbed this mountain many times;
your mental map now returning,
remembering a trail that will lead us
up through the bare rubble
of this erupted mountainside.

There are always many reasons for doing something.
We shuffle, split the deck and shuffle the reasons again,
trying to place what should be on top
even when we are certain
the wrong card may turn up.

I say: I want to brag
that I faced death on a volcano so active
it's still smoking, one to which
so many lives have been lost
some bodies still haven't been found.

You have been feeding me pieces of disasters.
Taste this: a train hurtling toward the washed-out bridge.
Swallow that: an entire class plunged to their deaths.
Everywhere we went this weekend,
you have told a story of death, disaster or terror.
I think this is why I could follow you anywhere.

Almost at the summit, I am crying
because of the pain in my legs. I know I can't
catch up so I stop and look around:
on a clear day there would have been an amazing view,
today all that is offered is velvety shades of grey
and the faint blue smudge of your jacket waiting for me.

When I reach the summit, you hand me a sandwich.
The steaming crater lake has my attention
and I announce that I want to put my hand in it.
It is sulphuric, you say, it will eat your skin right off.
I don't know if I believe you but I stay away.

As you lead me to the emergency hut,
you tell me about nine men who died in the original
when this mountain erupted two years ago.
I want to kiss you, reach up, deal a short warm embrace.
I know this is impossible so I touch your rain jacket instead.

It begins to rain, cold and sharp.
I am still holding my sandwich so you zip up my jacket,
tie up my hood, unaware your fingers graze my cheek.
You tell me we must hurry and we begin our descent.

Suddenly a new person,
I run down the mountain, skip over rocks,
slip on the lahar, slide down the patch of summer snow.

This mountain is mine, I feel it bowing under me.
I am flying down its face.

I don't realize until I see your face
that I have scraped my right leg,
the rain doing its best to wash away my blood
but it can't keep up and I am triumphant.
This is my badge, evidence of a winning hand.

The rain has changed the landscape;
waterfalls and strong streams have appeared out of nowhere,
nothing is recognizable but you seem to know
where we are going even through your steamed-over glasses,
so I follow you closely.

It takes us only half the time to descend
as it did to reach the summit and you are pleased
with our time. Back at the car we begin
peeling off our layers, now too wet to be useful.
Exhaustion has overcome us so we speak only in smiles.
Behind us, the mountain remains an invisible mass.

JUGGLERS' REST

Our lodging is run by jugglers,
people who throw knives, breathe fire,
do the impossible to earn a living.

There is a small pool, a large porch, boxes full of juggling toys
but we chose solace on the hammock, bare feet swinging
beneath a canopy heavy with ripening grapes.

Over dinner we are told of a couple yachting
nearby in the Sounds, last seen at a marina party
boarding a catamaran on a night just like tonight.

Two weeks of dragging the numerous bays and coves,
police searches, questions, media infatuation.
Things like this just don't happen here, everyone says.

We are told to be careful, to rethink our hitching plans—
they were local, young, our age, they tell us hands folded
   tightly in laps,
this is to mean something, more than it does to us.

The evening sky is painted pink and delicate and bright.
Sweetness from unfamiliar flowers permeates
and will be years before we are aware of its absence.

Blackness comes quickly and the sky is littered with foreign
   constellations.
For the first time I realize how far from everything I am
without the Big Dipper and the North Star to point my way.

Our hosts begin a show, balls of flames dance and fly—
huge circles sweeping high then low, popping like electric corn,
Tinkerbell on steroids weaving magic.

He asks for a volunteer and I walk over feet cool
on the silky dusted ground. He hands me an unlit torch, smiles,
eyes sparkling and tells me I am going to eat fire.

I practise twice, once hitting my teeth against the cool metal
and I realize how much this could hurt,
that flame and flesh are not the wisest of combinations,

but the torch is lit despite my apprehension.
I extend my arm high and straight,
bend my wrist bringing the flame's warmth to my face.

My mouth opens wider than any dentist has seen—
flame in and lips cover. I wait, eyes wide,
and expel slowly as my host had instructed.

There are no burns or blisters, nothing has changed
except for a strange taste on my tongue and a flickering inside
that feels stolen.

Melbourne

driving into Melbourne
smelling the storm ahead of you

sweet astringent

you want to pull at your nostrils
let the smell swallow you whole

you drive into the rain
the lightning pulsing above the city

a disco light

a bug zapper sucking the
42 degrees Centigrade

away from the heat-soaked
sponge cement the city is rising from

MAGNETIC ISLAND

I

I am on Magnetic Island, on the edge of Australia
in what is really the only bar on the island
with a man named Two Dogs,
an institution, but too much of an embarrassment
that the staff try to have him drunk and gone
by the time the tourists begin to arrive.
I have come too early and they are running behind
so I play a game of pool with this man
whose skin has been stained either by the sun or cigarette tar,
but whatever has coloured this man a yellowed brown,
has done damage even deeper
and I know he is dying.
If I had the luxury to rely on skill rather than chance,
I would have let Two Dogs win,
but I don't,
so I do try and I do win.
He pats me on the back and begins to tell me something
but his coughing overtakes him
so I walk away.

II

I am a tourist, a stranger,
this gives me the power
to turn my back on
anyone and anything.

III

Outside, a large sweating man holds up
a frog wrapped in a pink ribbon.
He coos to her
then barks to the crowd and the bidding begins.
A young man from Melbourne
buys me a drink without even asking if he may.
The older woman beside him glares at me,
I have interrupted her charms.

Perched on a barstool, her arm holds her drink extended—
this is her way of balancing.
I want to push her, tap her lightly on the shoulder.
But I am sure that later in the night
she will fall regardless of my actions.
The overweight man holds up another frog,
this one a purple ribbon,
and my man from Melbourne begins to bid.
He laughs and then whispers,
lips too close to my skin,
that he has no intention on betting,
he just lies to see how high the stakes can rise.
I smile and step back.
The frogs have been let go and the blue one wins.
A Canadian couple with a camcorder has won
and are squealing with disbelief. I thank
the Melbourne man for the drink that has yet to arrive
and I walk out of the lights
to the Moke I have rented
and drive.

IV

It is an island, a small island,
so I can't go far
and really, there is only one road.
But I want to drive,
drive away,
just go.

V

I pass Two Dogs walking up a hill.
I think for a moment I should stop,
deliver him home, but I have no desire
to become that connected.
I drive to the highest point possible
and put on the brake. I sit there
and on one side I see
the lights of Townsville across the water,
on the mainland.

I rev the motor breaking the silence around me.
On the other is blackness,
open water,
all possibilities.

VI

I am sitting on the edge of
this continent ready to slip
drown in the warm Pacific
my body caught on the living skeletons
the vibrant coral
floating bloated, ballooned, waiting for another tourist
to swim by, unhook me, and let me fall to the depths.

This is what I want.

Acknowledgements

Some of these poems have appeared in the following publications: *Border Crossings*, *CV2*, *The Dalhousie Review*, *Event*, *Grain*, *Larger Than Life: An Anthology of Celebrity* (Black Moss Press, 2002), *learning to breathe* (above/ground press, 1996), *Pagitica*, *Prairie Fire*, *Windsor Review* and in a broadsheet published by Greenboathouse Books. My thanks to the editors and publishers of each.

My sincere gratitude to the many who have contributed to these poems along the way, especially George McWhirter, Nancy Lee and Aurian Haller. I am forever indebted to Jennica Harper, Jeff Morris and Laisha Rosnau for their invaluable insights, brilliant commentary and warm friendships.

In addition to those above, I'd like to thank Madeleine Thien, Lee Henderson, Steve and Lara Galloway, Charlotte Gill, Kevin Chong, Heather Frechette, Rick Maddocks, Cindy Reid and Tara Deans for their treasured friendships and continued support.

Thank you to Caitlin Press and to the Canada Council of the Arts.

Many thanks to my family for their immeasurable support and love: my parents Gwen and Manfred Dachsel; my two sisters, real and chosen, Karena Dachsel and Denise Hrynkewich; my in-laws George and Carol Kerr; and to my gorgeous son Atticus.

And above all, thank you to my dear husband Kevin who is a million things to me. My compass, my love, my perfect travelling companion: none of this would have been possible without you.

MARITA DACHSEL was born and raised in Williams Lake, BC, and has lived in Kamloops, Dawson City, Auckland and Montpellier, France. She has an MFA in Creative Writing from UBC and has been published widely in Canadian literary journals. She currently lives in Vancouver with her husband, playwright Kevin Kerr, and their son, Atticus.